Scott Pattison

W9-CDE-433

Also by Tony Campolo

Partly Right
A Reasonable Faith
It's Friday, but Sunday's Coming'
You Can Make a Difference
Who Switched the Price Tags?
20 Hot Potatoes Christians Are Afraid to Touch
The Kingdom of God Is a Party

with Bart Campolo
Things We Wish We Had Said

HOW TO BE
PENTECOSTAL

Without Speaking in Tongues

TONY CAMPOLO

HOW TO BE

PENTECOSTAL

Without Speaking in Tongues

WORD PUBLISHING

Dallas · London · Vancouver · Melbourne

How to Be Pentecostal Without Speaking in Tongues

Copyright © 1991 by Anthony Campolo. All rights reserved. No portion of this book may be reproduced in any form, except for brief quotations in reviews, without written permission from the publisher.

Scripture quotations are from the King James Version.

Library of Congress Cataloging-in-Publication Data:

Campolo, Anthony.
    How to be Pentecostal without speaking in tongues / Anthony Campolo.
        p.   cm.
    ISBN 0-8499-0884-1
    1. Holy Spirit.   2. Pentecostalism.   I. Title.
    BT121.2.C25   1991
    234'.13—dc20   91-17220
                                                                CIP

1 2 3 4 9   AGF   9 8 7 6 5 4 3

Printed in the United States of America

To my charismatic baby granddaughter

Miranda Sarah Campolo

Contents

Introduction

This is a book about the most important thing going on in the world—the work of the Holy Spirit.

It is almost impossible to go anywhere in Christendom these days without coming across some evidence of the growing Charismatic movement. In Latin America it is sweeping people into Pentecostal churches in phenomenal numbers. In England there is constant talk of the "signs and wonders" of the Kingdom of God that are being wrought under the power of the Spirit. Across the United States Pentecostal churches are growing in leaps and bounds even as mainline churches shift into rapid decline. This book is about these remarkable movements of the Spirit.

Some of what goes on under the name of the Charismatic movement has become known as the Renewal movement. Staid churches are experiencing new vitality as the Spirit blows away the cobwebs that gathered during their more lethargic days. Young people are being challenged to be missionaries and evangelists in record numbers. New forms of worship are waking people up to new joys on Sunday morning. Small groups are forming that are providing mutual love and support for persons who hitherto felt weak and alone.

1

But there is a downside to all of this. Like any good thing that comes from God there are abuses by those who want to use the things of God for selfish purposes. There are phonies who are gaining wealth and prestige by claiming to have special gifts from God. And there are practices that hide behind the guise of being initiated by the Holy Spirit, but they are nothing more than the cheap tricks of charlatans.

This book is an attempt to help the uninitiated to understand what is going on in this wonderful, mystical, exciting, dangerous, and confusing world of the emerging Charismatic movement. It is an attempt to clarify what is happening; to provide a handle on some of the terms and vocabulary used by charismatics; and to perceive what is real and what is phony. Most importantly, however, these pages should spell out for those who are not charismatics how the Spirit becomes a dynamic presence in the lives of those Christians who know that there is more to being a Christian than just believing the right doctrines and practicing the right rituals.

The Holy Spirit always upsets the status quo. The Spirit disrupts the old order of things and ushers in a new openness. The Spirit is the new wine in the old wineskins and the new cloth on the old garment. Those who want everything to remain as it was ought not to get involved with the things of the Spirit, because the ministry of the Spirit makes all things new: "Therefore if any man be in Christ, he is a new creature: old things are passed away; behold, all things are become new" (2 Cor. 5:17).

The Charismatic Movement

Chapter 1

Something's Blowin' in the Wind

Pentecostalism just isn't what it used to be, at least so far as outsiders are concerned. Those in the mainstream churches no longer view the Charismatic movement as laughable "holy-rollers" pumped into uncontrolled hysterics by semi-charlatans. Such images, if they were ever true, have been more than obliterated by members of their own congregations who have been changed in positive ways by the so-called infilling of the Spirit. There are just too many Presbyterians, Episcopalians, and Roman Catholics who talk of spiritual deliverance and physical healing for there to be a broad denial that something good and miraculous is taking place across the land and around the world. The evidence is obvious.

Several years ago I visited a small town in the Dominican Republic (let us call it El Sebo) in order to meet with a faithful fundamentalist minister who was serving there. The town was a mess in every sense. Trash was everywhere. Garbage clogged the open sewers. Bodies of stripped cars cluttered every vacant lot, and the houses of the town seemed tumbled down, dirty, and neglected. It was one of those poor towns that elicits pity for those who are destined to make it their home.

The missionary whom I visited talked about how little progress he had seen during more than a decade of ministry. There were less than a dozen people who belonged to his little church. And this handful of Christians worked very hard to keep from falling back into the cesspool of degradation that seemed evident everywhere around them. The bars and cantinas of the town did a hefty business, and drunkenness was common. Perhaps the only thing that might have been more common than drunkenness was sexual promiscuity. The young men of the town were anxious to prove their machismo and worked overtime trying to hustle every available female into bed. The old men talked with a strange kind of reluctant pride of the many children around town that they had fathered out of wedlock. The official religion of the town was Roman Catholic, but the real religion was a combination of some folk myths and superstitions mixed with voodoo.

To say the least, El Sebo was depressing. The missionary was discouraged. He seemed to be doing little more than going though the motions of evangelizing and teaching. And he had seemingly little expectation that anything good would come from his efforts.

"God will judge us for our faithfulness, not for our success," he reminded me. That being true, this dear saint of God was sure to be judged faithful on that final day when we all stand before the Eternal Throne, for being faithful was about all he was.

"What this town needs is a revival!" he declared to me. "Only God Himself coming down and performing a miracle can change things around here."

And I readily agreed.

A little over four years later I had an occasion to revisit El Sebo. And when I arrived in town I was overtaken immediately with the obvious evidence of change. "Maybe the sun is shining brighter today," I said to myself. "Maybe I remember things as being worse than they really were. Perhaps these seemingly happy people greeting each other with friendly smiles were really not as beaten down as my memory pictured them. Maybe my perception of things was mistaken."

The streets were relatively free of trash and debris. I didn't see any drunks around. The houses seemed to have a bright, scrubbed look about them. To tell the truth, El Sebo did not seem to be all that bad a place to live and raise a family.

When I caught up with my missionary friend he assured me it was not my imagination. He explained that it was not only the way the town looked that was different, the people themselves were changed.

"The drinking has dropped off," he reported. "The young people are not doing many of the immoral things they used to do, so there aren't many teenage girls becoming pregnant. I'll even have to admit that many people are married now who just used to live together before."

The economy of El Sebo had changed too. The onetime feeble coffee business was prospering because the workers had eliminated their middle man. They had gotten together and chipped in to buy their own truck and were delivering their coffee to the market themselves. Their increased income apparently had stimulated the development of better coffee plants, and the creation of a co-op had enabled them to challenge the exploitive practices of the old general store. Their growing coffee industry had spun off at least ten to fifteen cottage industries, which in turn had created jobs for scores of the townspeople. El Sebo might be something less than it should be, but it was certainly a far cry from what it used to be.

My missionary friend explained the cause for all of these changes. "It's the priest," he said, with a bit of anger in his voice. "That priest went down to Santo Domingo and got wrapped up with some Charismatics. When he got back here, he worked overtime spreading all of that false doctrine, and the people bought what he told them. His church is packed now, not only for Sun-

9

day masses, but two or three times during the week for those praise services he holds. He's made half of this town into Charismatics, and El Sebo just isn't the same anymore."

"You don't seem to be pleased by all of this," I responded.

"Why should I be?" was his retort. "All of these seemingly good things that you see happening are only Satan's way of confusing people and getting more of them into that deceptive Pentecostalism."

He went on to explain how he believed that all that was going on under the leadership of that charismatic priest was nothing more than a cover-up for the "sneaky work of the Evil One." It was his opinion that Satan knew that "real" revival was about to break out in that town and had started this Charismatic movement to keep it from happening.

I couldn't believe my ears. Did he really believe that Satan had done all of this good just to keep the people of that town from getting converted to his Dispensationalist theology? Could he see all the changes that were taking place around him and honestly not attribute them to God? Of course the answer to these questions is *yes!*

When Jesus was confronted by those who saw his good works and then attributed them to Satan, He declared,

> . . . Every kingdom divided against itself is brought to desolation; and every city or house divided against itself shall not stand: and if Satan cast out Satan, he is divided against himself; how shall then his kingdom stand? And if I by Beelzebub cast out devils, by whom do your children cast them out? therefore they shall be your judges. But if I cast out devils by the Spirit of God, then the Kingdom of God is come unto you.
>
> *Matthew 12:25–28*

I was so startled by my friend's judgment that I failed to give him the warning that Jesus gave to those who could look at the works of the Holy Spirit and not recognize them:

10

Either make the tree good, and his fruit good; or else make the tree corrupt, and his fruit corrupt: for the tree is known by his fruit. O generation of vipers, how can ye, being evil, speak good things? for out of the abundance of the heart the mouth speaketh.

Matthew 12:33

Across Latin America the Charismatic movement is bringing millions into a changed and holy lifestyle. In Australia, New Zealand, and the United Kingdom the flames of a charismatic revival are beginning to burn. There are healings and miracles reported everywhere. Pentecostal churches have become the fastest growing churches in America. We cannot deny what the facts reveal. The Charismatic movement has become the most dynamic expression of Christianity in the world today.

On the other hand, I am not denying that there have been abuses and that some strange things have gone on in the name of Pentecostalism. The scriptures do commend us to be discerning about what is going on in the name of the Holy Spirit: "Beloved, believe not every spirit, but try the spirits whether they are of God: because many false prophets are gone out into the world" (1 John 4:1). It is a Christian responsibility to examine what is going on in all facets of this growing religious phenomenon. This is particularly important at a time when there is so much phoniness and deception in Pentecostalism.

As a case in point, there was a well-known West Coast preacher who claimed to possess all kinds of charismatic powers. During revivals and crusades he exercised one of these powers by being able to pick out people in the audience who had some very specific problems or physical ailments. He then could proceed to "prophesy" solutions to those problems and pronounce healings for those whom he picked out as having specific sicknesses and infirmities. With his face strained and his eyes closed he would say something like: "There is someone here tonight whose sister in Fresno, California is suffering with cancer. God wants to heal

11

your sister so that she can go on raising her three young daughters and her new baby boy. You know who you are. Would you please stand so that we can lay hands on you and pray for her recovery?"

Then some befuddled man would stand and, with tears streaming down his cheeks, cry out, "It's me! Oh, Reverend, please pray for my sister and please pray for me!"

The detailed specifics about the sick woman would leave little doubt in anyone's mind that this charismatic evangelist had a special gift of discernment from God. There would be "Ohs" and "Ahs" of amazement throughout the crowd. As he worked his magic the miraculous appeared to be happening right before their eyes. People could not help but be impressed.

The fame and fortune of this particular evangelist grew nightly. The offering plates were constantly filled. The crowds regularly grew in numbers. He was, as they say, "on a roll."

Then came the exposé. One cynical member of the congregation noticed that the evangelist had a hearing aid. He wondered why a man with such a great gift of healing could not take care of his own particular problem.

His suspicions were confirmed when he brought a high-frequency radio receiver to a subsequent meeting and was able to intercept messages that the evangelist's wife was sending him from a back room. What was really happening was that prior to the start of the meeting, the evangelist's wife mingled with the crowd and picked up specific information about various people in the audience. She would ask questions and overhear conversations. Later, when the evangelist was in the midst of his performance, she would radio this information to him. As he walked up and down the aisles of the auditorium preaching and "healing," she would feed him the facts he needed to look like someone with a direct line to God.

What made matters worse was that this particular evangelist was exposed on Johnny Carson's "Tonight Show." The man who had figured out what was going on had made recordings of the radio conversations he intercepted between the evangelist and his wife, and he played them for the entertainment of millions of American television viewers. Carson mockingly remarked how God's voice and the voice of the evangelist's wife were almost identical. The audience laughed, but many of us who believe in a God who can perform miracles were in pain. It is always painful to those of the church when one of their members is publicly disgraced. "Whether one member suffer, all the members suffer with it" (1 Cor. 12:26).

Not all phoniness in the Charismatic movement is quite so blatant and purposefully deceptive. Let me give you an example of how a well-meaning person can hurt the integrity of legitimate Pentecostalism.

It has been almost a decade since I was the speaker for an unusual graduation service in Washington, D.C. Some men had come to know Christ as personal Savior and Lord while in prison, and they had completed a training course to equip them to be more effective witnesses while continuing to serve their time behind bars. I had spent some time with these men the afternoon preceding the evening graduation. I had heard their painful stories and was a bit broken by the tragedies they related to me.

One man had raped a seventeen-year-old girl who had lived down the street from him. He was a Christian now, but his wife and children, nevertheless, had refused to forgive him and never wanted to see him again.

Another man was guilty of armed robbery. His elderly mother was now dying of cancer and was crying to see him before she died, but he could not go to her.

Another had severely beaten his wife and children, but in spite of his professed conversion they had rejected him and had taken someone else to be the husband and father for the family.

The stories went on and on, heartbreak after heartbreak, tragedy after tragedy.

During the graduation exercises and just before I was to speak, a woman rose to sing. She was the special music for the program. But before she sang she said, "There are just a few words I'd like to share with you before I sing." I wish she hadn't.

"On the way over here tonight," she said, "I was driving my new station wagon. It's less than two weeks old. I was driving right behind a big truck carrying a load of stones. One of the stones fell off the truck, hit the highway, bounced up, and hit my windshield. It put a nick in the glass. I was so depressed.

"When I got out of the car to come in here, I put my finger on that nick and prayed a simple prayer that God would heal it. And would you believe that when I removed my finger that nick was gone?"

"No," mumbled several of the men in an all too audible manner.

The woman, embarrassed that her healing-of-the-windshield story had not gone over better, cleared her throat and proceeded to sing.

These are only two examples, but these sorts of abuses and trivializations of the work of the Holy Spirit have given the Charismatic movement a bad name. We must not, however, allow some phonies and some sincere but misguided persons to turn us off to what may be an era of unusual outpourings of the Holy Spirit. We must not let abuses blind us to some of the greatest blessings the world has seen since Pentecost.

Chapter 2

How Did Something So Strange Get So Popular?